are accomplished, that I will punish the King of Babylon, and so we have it in the 13th verse of this chapter, "I have raised him up in righteousness, and I will direct all his ways and he shall build my city, and he shall let go my captives, not for price nor reward, saith the Lord of hosts." Now all this came to pass just according unto the Word of the Lord by his servants. Thus it is written "Now in the first year of Cyrus, King of Persia, he made a proclamation throughout all his kingdom, and put it also in writing, saying, "Thus saith Cyrus, King of Persia, all the kingdoms of the earth hath the Lord God of heaven given me, and He hath charged me to build Him an house in Jerusalem, which is in Judah, who is there among you of all His people? The Lord his God be with him and let him go up!" 2 Chron., xxxvi., 22-23. When the proclamation of Cyrus was published it came upon the poor captive Jews so very sudden as to appear like a dream, "When the Lord turned again the captivity of Zion, we were like them that dream." They could hardly tell whether it was a real thing or a vision, the news was so great and so good, too good to be true. Oh how astounding is the breaking forth of divine mercy on behalf of the chosen. Nature cannot credit the report, only faith, even the faith of God's elect, which is the gift of God, can embrace tidings of peace. When they, as it were, came to themselves and so perceived the fact of that they heard, they said "Then was our mouth filled with laughter, and our tongue with singing." Now they that had formerly been drunken with sorrow sitting down by the rivers of Babylon weeping in bitterness swelling as it were, the flowing stream with their tears, having cast their harps upon the willows, having no heart to make use of them, now in the days of prosperity found use both for their tongue and harp, they sing the songs of

Zion. "The singers went before, the players on instruments follow after," they shout "the Lord hath done great things for us, whereof we are glad." Thus the Lord delivered His Israel by the hand of Cyrus. Now in this account is there no vein of spiritual truth? Yes! blessed be God there is, for at the 8th verse, "Drop down ye heavens from above, and let the skies pour down righteousness, let the earth open and let them bring forth salvation, and let righteousness spring up together, I, the Lord have created it." These words do not fit Cyrus so well, as our most glorious Christ. And it is thus the Holy Ghost, by His servant the prophet, leads us from Cyrus to Christ, from the Type to the Anti-Type, from the temporal redemption of the Jews, to the spiritual redemption of the Lord's people. The Redeemer in his divine nature came from heaven, He was the Lord from heaven, and yet made of a woman in the lowest parts of the earth. Thus the "Rod that came forth out of the stem of Jesse, and the branch that grew out of his roots, became beautiful and glorious, and the fruit of the earth excellent and comely for them that are escaped of Israel." Not beautiful and glorious, and the fruit of the earth excellent and comely in the estimation of all men. To some He is as a root out of a dry ground, he hath no form or comeliness. But to them who by the revelation of Him in them by the Holy Ghost, have escaped the wrath of God, to such He is indeed glorious and precious. Now may the Lord the Holy Spirit direct our minds to the glorious things of the grace of God, enfolded in the words I first read, "I will go before thee, etc."

FIRST. The Lord has gone before his people.

SECONDLY. The good things He will do for them.

First. The Lord has gone before his people. Yes, blessed be His precious name, and the desire of their souls is towards Him; the secret wish of their souls is to follow after Him. The Holy Ghost stirs them up and inspires them to this, "Then shall we know if we follow on to know the Lord, His going is prepared as the morning, and He shall come unto us as the rain, as the latter and former rain unto the earth," Hosea vi., 3. No man can follow after the Lord except God by the spirit of regeneration first turn the heart from death to life, and from sin to holiness. The Lord thrust out the great apostle into His vineyard, to do his work, and He was with him in that work, "Delivering him from the people, and from the Gentiles unto whom He sent Him," "To open their eyes, and to turn them from darkness to light, and from the power of Satan unto God." When under the power of Satan, the things agreeable and congenial with that spirit is followed after, "Wherein in times past ye walked according to the course of this world, according to the prince of the power of the air, the spirit that now worketh in the children of disobedience." Even so when led by the influence of the Spirit of God, the heart follows after God. A gracious heart is at *times* under divine influence, puts forth desires, and endeavours in the use of all means to obtain a soul-comforting knowledge of God, and if some little is known and felt of God, as the God of grace, Oh how that soul does follow after more. "I press toward the mark, for the prize of the high calling of God in Christ Jesus." That which they do so earnestly follow after they will certainly obtain. Nothing can hinder it, God has fixed it, that the election shall obtain it. God who has begun in mercy with His people, He will go on; Come then ye poor, naked, worthless, vile, and guilty (spiritually so) follower of the Lord. The Lord is before you, fear not, hope thou in God for thou shalt yet praise Him, He will be found of thee, He is a rewarder of them that diligently seek Him. Hebrews xi., 6.

SECONDLY. In the 22nd verse of this chapter, the Lord is set before the believer as the object of faith, " Look unto Me and be ye saved, all the ends of the earth, for I am God and there is none else." See the type of this in Num. xxi., the people spake against God and against Moses, "Wherefore have ye brought us up out of Egypt to die in the wilderness for there is no bread." When the people made confession of their sins, and requested Moses to intercede with God for them, the Lord commanded Moses to make a serpent of brass, and set it upon a pole, that it might be lifted up. And it came to pass that if a serpent had bitten any man when he beheld the serpent of brass he lived. To this the Saviour alludes, "And as Moses lifted up the serpent in the wilderness, even so must the Son of Man be lifted up, that whosoever believeth in Him should not perish, but have eternal life," John iii., 14—15. Lifted up as an object to be looked upon by the stung Israelites. Even so must the Son of Man, our most glorious Christ, be looked unto by faith, then the guilty sinner is healed, and shall not perish but have eternal life. The lifting up of the Son of Man signified the crucifixion of the Son of God. The faith of God's elect is that keen eye in the understanding of believers by which the hidden things of the grace of God is discerned. Let me address a word of encouragement to broken-hearted sinners stung with the guilt of sin, Jesus Christ the Lamb of God, that taketh away the sin of the world, is the object before you, and the deadly nature of sin is the pricking cause of your looking. Say not, you are too great a sinner or that the day of mercy is past, or that you are too unworthy. If a stung Israelite had such reasoning in him, and acting on it, turned his eyes downward he would have perished. God has made you feel the malady, on purpose to prepare you for the remedy. Poor Jonah in his great extremity said, "I am cast out of Thy sight, yet will I look again toward Thy Holy Temple," Jonah ii., 4. And you know he did not look in vain for God delivered him. Oh blessed tidings, look unto me ye poor creatures at the ends of the earth, ye that are ready to perish, come cast your languid eye to that spectacle of woe transfixed on the cross, look to Him, that ye may live by Him, Gal. ii., 20. Look to Him that ye may be like Him, 2 Cor. iii., 18. Look to Him that ye may loathe sin, Ezek. xxxvi., 31.

THIRDLY. He has gone before His people as a glorious breaker, as we find in Micah, "The breaker is come up before them, they have broken up, and have passed through the gate, and are gone out by it, and their King shall pass before them, and the Lord on the head of them," Micah ii., 13.

The great and glorious work this Almighty breaker came to do was, to demolish the strongholds of Satan. "For this purpose, the Son of God was manifested that he might destroy the works of the Devil," 1 John, iii., 8. His coming and appearing in human nature did not make Him the Son of God but He was manifested in it. Nothing short of the Eternal Son of God in the likeness of sinful flesh could destroy death, and him that had the power over death. Death entered by sin, the guilt of sin brought it in, and in this is Satan's interest; by this gate he came into the world; had there been no sin to let him in, he would have had no more to do in the world than in heaven. Then what a hideous monster must sin be, " Pregnant cause of misery." What an act of condescension even to eternal admiration, that the Son of Man should take human nature, that therein He might, as the mighty God, break down and break through all the power of sin, death, Satan, and hell, and that by death, the fruit of sin (for as the Surety sin was laid upon Him) was borne by Him for which He was wounded, bruised, and died. Now this of all others seemed the most contrary way. Virtually in His death and resurrection all the opposing powers have been for ever defeated, and in the actual application of it unto the conscience of the redeemed the dominion of sin and Satan is demolished. Our blessed Redeemer, the Samson of the New Testament, in His death pulled down the palace of Satan about his ears. In dying, Oh wonderful ! He conquered all foes, and subdued all things to Himself. When men and devils thought they had destroyed Him, God in Him and by Him, destroyed them. Blessed mystery it is set before us, and at times we rejoice in the meditation of it.

FOURTHLY. He goes before His people in His ministers directing them in their ministry, as to the matter of their subjects. Their heart and tongue are the Lord's. The Lord does in a marvellous way take possession of heart and tongue, that they can neither think their own thoughts, or speak their own words. Some of the Lord's servants have laboured hard in private, in much study have framed a sermon and have felt sweetness in their own soul, in putting the same together, thinking it was the will of God that the matter springing up in the heart in private should be proclaimed upon the housetop. But to their surprise, what to them was so sweet in private meditation, has been, when in the pulpit, swept from the mind, as if it had never been there,

and they left standing before the people in a feeling of confusion, the mind void of matter. Oh how they have trembled at such times not knowing what to say. A trying position indeed. Thinking every moment their mouth would be stopped but they have kept on saying something which, to them, has seemed nothing more than a mass of confusion. They have left the pulpit ashamed and vexed, fearing to see or speak to anyone, their poor soul cast down ; in their thinking they have laboured in vain, and have spent their strength for naught. But behold the wise and gracious hand of God has been in it all, taking from them their well-ordered sermon, and leaving them to wander in their discourse that thereby the case of some poor trembling fearing soul may be traced out to their comfort and peace.

Not a few of the Lord's family have in this way been much surprised, their trials in soul matters, and that which befell them outwardly, together with their fears and temptations, have been spoken of, and so minutely described, as if the minister had known all about their individual case. The Lord thus goes before His people in shutting up His ministers and laying them, as it were, in irons, that they may speak to those poor souls that are in the horrible pit. For poor dear souls, some of them are so plagued with sin, guilt, fears, and desperate risings of infidelity, they think there never were such strange beings as they feel themselves among the Lord's people. When the servant of the Lord is driven out of his own track into a strange path (for so it appears to him) as he feels so he speaks (for God's ministers speak out of an exercised heart), if in bonds they speak of bonds, describing both the fetters, prison, and dungeon. If guilt press heavily upon them, they set before the people true conviction of sin, pointing out the various workings of the mind under it, and the death warrant that attends it. If bowed down with fears, and faith so weak and withered, not being able to lay hold of the promise, they speak of fears and the sinking of the soul under them. Soldiers of the cross must meet with opposition on every hand, temptations to leave the work, darkness, bound up in spirit, every spiritual thought scattered. The Bible sealed, unbelief prevalent; in such a storm God sometimes sends his ministers in their feelings driven up and down, fearing they will prove an outcast on purpose to pick up a poor deserted wretch just ready to perish. Thus the minister is in misery, yet preaching comfort to others. Cast down himself, yet lifting others up. Weak himself, a strength to others. Having nothing, yet abundantly giving unto others. Thus he takes the stumbling block out of the way of others. Yet he himself is stumbling upon the dark mountains. God's ministers speak as moved by the Holy Ghost, as he works in the mind under their varied crosses. None can preach to profit souls in any other way, for a preacher must lead the flock.

It was so with the Redeemer, He is set before us as the Apostle and High Priest of our profession, Heb. iii., 1. In this character, as sent of God, the Spirit of the Lord God was upon Him, Isa. lxi., 1-2-3. Whereby he was enabled to preach good tidings unto the meek, to bind up the broken-hearted, to proclaim liberty to the captives, and opening of the prison to those that are bound. Moreover he had experience of the trials, temptations, and sufferings of believers. "For we have not an High Priest which cannot be touched with the feeling of our infirmities, but was in all points tempted like as we are, yet without sin, Heb. iv., 15. The apostle lays great stress upon this, signifying that from thence he was partly qualified to speak a word in season to him that is weary, Isa. l., 4. For in that He himself hath suffered, being tempted He is able to succour them that are tempted, Heb. ii., 18. It is indeed wonderful that the Blessed and Holy Redeemer, who was no less a person than the Eternal Son of the Eternal Father in human nature, should Himself condescend to such weakness, sorrows, and miseries of human nature, when under the assaults of temptation he was tried thereby, keenly felt it, and will always bear it in mind.

And notwithstanding He is now upon His throne of eternal peace and glory, He sees His poor brethren labouring in that storm in which He himself did so much business when He was upon earth, in prayers and supplications with strong crying and tears, unto His Father, Heb. v., 7. He is moved with compassion to their relief and succour—the proper effect of mercy and compassion. It sets power at work for the relief of them whose condition it is affected with. This my brethren is (and may the Lord bless it to your souls) the ability ascribed to our High Priest. Compassion and mercy arising from an experience of the sufferings of His people under temptations. He will put forth His power for the relief of His dear tempted ones. Thus He has gone before them in the ministration of His grace.

FIFTHLY. He goes before them in sufferings in which He is a leader unto them by example, so saith the apostle Peter. "Christ hath suffered for us leaving us an example that we should follow His steps." The children of God are sometimes ready to think it strange that they should fall into calamity and distress. Gideon seemed in a fix, when the angel told him "The Lord was with him," he replied "Whence is all this evil come upon us." What a riddle, the Lord with us and yet in such distress. Our enemies more numerous and powerful than we, "Surely the Lord hath forsaken us." This is just the language of Zion when in suffering circumstances but "Zion saith, the Lord hath forsaken me, and my Lord hath forgotten me." Poor Zion in her distress is ready to faint. Such things may befall us as we journey through this desert land to weary and burden us to an extent, so as to solicit us to give up all profession of the Gospel. Satan's aim is to make us heartless, desponding, and weary of the cross. Therefore says that wonderful cross-bearer, the apostle of the Gentiles, "For consider Him that endureth such contradictions of sinners against Himself, lest ye be weary and faint in your minds, Heb. xii., 3. Consider Him, ponder the matter between Him and us, He is the head we the body. If He suffered and endured such things, why should not His members partake of the same, in measure. Remember He was the Son of God, all power and glory was in His hand. Yet notwithstanding all His glory and power He trod the weary path of suffering to the extent of sufferings, and is set down at the right hand of God. Now, cast together this with yourselves, as the apostle has done before, and it will stand thus, "If so be that we suffer with Him, that we may be glorified together, Rom. viii., 17.

Christ passed through this world to sanctify it as a place of suffering and service. He had no constant residence here as His resting place. So the followers of Christ must be like affected, we must pass through the world as strangers. As He was in the world so must we expect to be. His kingdom is not of this world, John xviii., 36. It is not like the kingdom of this world of pomp, but a kingdom of patience and suffering. Let no Christian flatter himself of an easy passage to heaven, seeing that he is a follower of the

suffering Lamb of God, and "Of them who by faith and patience inherit the promises." The love and care of God of us, and toward us, is manifested in providing examples for us in the volume of truth. Hastily looking at the difficulties and oppositions from without and within, that we have to conflict with, we may be ready to think it impossible we shall be successfully brought through them and come off safe at last. The intention of the Holy Ghost, by His servant Paul, in the xi. of Hebrews is to remove this despondency in that long series of examples which he gives us. For there it is undeniably proved, by instances of all sorts, that faith will carry men, most blessedly, through the greatest difficulties they can possibly meet with in the profession, and obedience of it.

But then my dear brethren let us not forget one essential point that is required, *that there be the* same Spirit in us. In vain should we encourage any following or imitating of them who hath not the same spirit and principal. For thus the apostle speaks, " We having the same spirit of faith according as it is written, I believe, therefore have I spoken ; we also believe, and therefore speak," 2 Cor. iv., 13. So the apostle James, " Take my brethren, the prophets who have spoken in the name of the Lord, for an example of suffering, affliction, and of patience." If we share the same grace, and in the same love of God, go to the same heaven as the prophets who have spoken in the name of the Lord, we must expect to participate in their afflictions. If God makes us like them in glory, He will make us like them in suffering and patience. In all your tribulations, trials, and sufferings this is your consolation. You have the lot of His people, being bound up in the same bundle of honour with them. All those happy souls that are now at rest with God in glory, as having inherited the promises, were sometimes as we are, conflicting with corruptions and temptations, undergoing reproaches and persecutions, labouring in a constant course of obedience unto God. If then by grace we follow them in their work, we shall not fail to partake with them in their reward. Fear not thou suffering saint "It is thy Father's good pleasure to give thee the kingdom," and in somewhat similar manner as He, the Redeemer, entered into His glory. "Ought not Christ to have suffered these things and to enter into His glory." Thus He has gone before His church as a pattern of suffering.

The trials, troubles, and afflictions of the saints is no barren stock, they yield fruit, good fruit, sweet fruit, wholesome fruit, even the peaceable fruit of righteousness, Heb. xii., 11. In the proper and due season that which appears uncomely and distasteful in the bud, will be pleasant and sweet in the fruit. The whole of God's dealings and designs herein is set forth in a beautiful allusion to a husbandman in the management of his land, "Sow to yourselves in righteousness, reap in mercy, break up your fallow-ground, for it is time to seek the Lord, till He come and rain righteousness upon you," Hosea x., 12. What a filthy barren place is the heart of man, no fallow-ground half so full of weeds, thorns, and briers. The fallow-ground must be first broken up by the plough, before it is in a fit state to receive the seeds. So the heart must by afflictions, which may be compared to a plough, be broken up. Doth the ploughman plough all day to sow, doth he open and break the clods of his ground? Isa. xxviii., 24. When God by afflictions purgeth His vine, it is that it may bear more fruit. When He dresseth His ground it shall bring forth herbs meet for Himself. By this therefore shall the iniquity of

Jacob be purged, and this is all the fruit to take away his sin, Isa. xxvii., 9. Come let us consider the matter a moment longer. We all have lurking in our breast that creature exalting but God hating principle, self-righteousness. Notwithstanding all the purging trials we have passed through, that root of bitterness is still in us, and if God did not often send forth the North wind of adversity, it would soon spread itself like a green bay tree, in our words, our thoughts, our prayers, and we should walk before God with a stiff neck. We know from the Word of Truth "That pride goeth before destruction, and a haughty spirit before a fall, Prov. xvi., 18. Such a spirit God hates, how vehement is His language with regard to it. They that look upon themselves as better than others, and who say "stand by thyself, come not near me, I am holier than thou, these are a smoke in my nose, a fire that burneth all day," Isa. lxv., 5. How very offensive to the Divine Being, as smoke to the eyes and nostrils. Surely he will cast such a despicable thing from him. Then again, " I hate, I despise your feasts, and I will not smell in your solemn assemblies," Amos v., 21. Let them band together in their will-worship conforming themselves to certain rules, which have an outward show of solemnity, yet God regards them not, thus He says " Your new moon, and your appointed feasts, my soul hateth, they are a trouble to me, I am weary to bear them," Isa. l., 14. Now is it not a mercy, let the furnace be ever so hot, to be purified from such a proud God insulting principle? How very different the case with the church, as set forth coming out of the wilderness like pillars of smoke, perfumed with myrrh, and frankincense, with all powers of the merchant, Song iii., 6.

The wilderness is a place of trial, sorrow, fear, and distress ; desertion is the believer's lot when treading in the desolate wilderness, tears of sorrow drop from the eyes, sighs go up from the heart as a sacrifice with which God is well pleased, for they have been mixed with faith in the Lord Jesus Christ. In answer He grants His presence, then up comes the poor afflicted one from sorrow, the affections ascending like the perfume of incense, a pillar of smoke, and of mercy. Therefore we sometimes rejoice in tribulation.

But I come now to notice the second thing proposed, the removing every difficulty.

SECONDLY. Make the crooked places straight. How are we to understand this? We ought to bear in mind there are two sides to God's Truth. That side towards God, and that side towards us, or in other words, doctrine and experience. These two must be observed in explaining the truth, if not, we soon get into confusion in our ideas. Now God never did lead His people into a crooked path, that is, crooked to His purpose, His word, His love, wisdom, or grace. Let this rule be applied to all His providential or gracious dealings with His people, and they will be found to be straight therewith. "I will cause you to walk by the rivers of waters in a straight way, wherein they shall not stumble," Jere. xxxi., 9. Here we have a straight way in which God will cause His people to walk. Then again it is plainly expressed "Who worketh all things after the council of His own will," Eph. i., 11. Just as He pleases. Not a wild perverse, confused way, but in a wise and prudent manner, in the best way that can be devised, for He is wonderful in council, and excellent in working. I lead (is the language of wisdom) in the way of righteousness, in the midst of the paths of judgment. Blessed doctrine this, sweet comfort, when faith can lay hold of it the soul then

rejoices therein, and in humble confidence exclaims, Although my path to me is crooked and opposite in the extreme, it is straight with my Lord who is my Leader, Guide, and Counsellor, and He will make it plain. Then dejected soul fear not, God does not work in you, or without you, according to your fears, mistrust, or suspicions, but according to His wise councils. And shall not the Judge of all the earth do right, Gen. xviii., 25. He is too wise to err. Then we may say in confidence, God never in reality leads his people in a crooked way. This is the case as it regards doctrine, and doctrine is the foundation. The Lion of the tribe of Judah, the Root of David hath prevailed to open the book, and loose the seven seals thereof, Rev. v., 5.

> His providence unfolds the book,
> And makes His counsels shine,
> Each opening leaf and every stroke,
> Fulfils some deep design.

You will, I have no doubt, from my observation, understand my meaning, that in the whole course of a Christian's life, from the first step in grace to glory, there is not one crook therein, but that everything that falls out in their pilgrimage, is straight with the mind, will, and counsel of God. But how different the case at some seasons in the experience of the tried family of God. To their flesh and blood principles there is nothing but crooks both within and without, crooks before them, crooks behind them, crooks in the business, crooks in the family, crooks in their connection among friends, indeed look were they may nothing but crooks. Yet the apostle in his admonition sets the matter straight, " My brethren count it all joy when ye fall into divers temptations, knowing this that the trying of your faith worketh patience," James i., 2-3. Afflictions come by the direction of God for the trial of faith, that is the aim of God in your affliction, not destruction, but trial by afflictions, by crosses, by crooked things arising one after another, you are purified and made white, Dan. xi., 35. God ordains the troubles of believers in such manner as to be productive of three things.

FIRST. The bringing to light the evils of the carnal heart, which is the scum and dross, Ezek. xxii., 20.

SECONDLY. To discern and bring to light that grace implanted in the heart. When He hath tried me I shall come forth as gold, Job. xxiii., 10. That is, the grace of God in me will in the end shine out, precious, honourable, weighty, durable, and desirable.

THIRDLY. The faithfulness of God will in them be manifested. God is faithful, who will not suffer you to be tempted above that ye are able to bear, but will with the temptation also make a way to escape, 1 Cor. x., 13. God determines to give strength according to the day of trial, and He proportions the afflictions to the strength He gives. He will never leave them, nor forsake them, but will bear, and carry, and save them unto the uttermost, and they shall hold on, and out, unto the end. Let us just for a moment observe some of those things that are crooks to the believer.

FIRST. What a crook it is to a believer to be always last. Make any progress in the divine life he cannot. The inward warfare between flesh and spirit, the opposition he meets from Satan, who is the accuser of the brethren, the chains of guilt which so often fetter his soul, fears and despondings, and heart failings, and mountains of difficulties that rise up, these things keep him upon the back-ground, he dare not come forth to the light. He is feeble and sore broken far behind. Paul saith, I press toward the mark

for the prize of the high calling of God in Christ Jesus, Phil. iii., 14. But this poor soul looks upon himself as fainting by the way, just upon the point of giving up everything of his profession as worthless. No Christian he thinks ever felt like him, dead, carnal, foolish, wandering in mind and heart far from God. This is a crook. God makes it plain and straight. By such things the Lord teaches the trembling one that the race is not to the swift, nor the battle to the strong. This reconciles the mind to the cross, removes the stumbling blocks, and makes straight that which was crooked before.

SECONDLY. Another crooked thing the Christian cannot put into practice. The good resolutions of his mind, his heart, will, and affections is set upon good, he loves it, tries to follow after, and is bent upon doing it. Yea, his heart is fixed, as he thinks, thereon. But the moment he sets about the performance thereof, then something starts up as a preventative. Sometimes a very trivial thing will do it, the things of a moment snatch away the mind from the important things of eternity. This is a crook, and the more the Christian reasons upon it the more crooked it appears. Surely if I was a true believer in Jesus Christ, things would be different, "For the kingdom of God is not in word but in power." Satan now steps forth as an accuser and lays many things to the charge of the soul ; see, says the tempter, there it is, if the fear of God was in you, it would be a fountain life to depart from the snares of death, Prov. xiv., 27. But you are always entangled in some snare, you are a stranger to delivering grace. The flesh, sin, and the world overcomes you, beats you down, overturns all your purposes and this proves you a servant of sin, "For of whom a man is overcome, of the same is he brought into bondage," and thus does the poor suffering one pass upon himself the fearful sentence of condemnation. This trial comes not by chance, but for good. The Lord intends it preparative to a blessing. There is in every Christian a principle to trust in *self*, and to make his fleshly purposes his aim, and could he perform those good works he intended to do, like many others, he would build a Babel tower to reach to heaven. Now the Lord by such things teaches him, his strength is not in himself. He is brought to the point, that he cannot put trust in himself, nor in anybody else, whenever he has placed his trust in man, he has met with disappointment. Whenever he has accepted anything from the creature nothing has followed but vexation, destroyed hopes, and blighted expectations. In the midst of these crooks the Lord in the powerful beams of His grace from off the mercy seat shines into his heart, which enlightens his understanding in the word. And now he clearly sees that Christ is to be his all. He now sees who, and what the Son of God is. And as faith sees Him, the soul rejoices in Him, hope anchors in Him. Ah, says the soul, He is worthy of all confidence. Thus the Lord makes this crooked thing straight.

THIRDLY. Another crooked thing, the way and manner in which God gives being, (or as it were) an existence to His promises. Believers are heirs of promise, Heb., vi. 17. The new covenant promises are their inheritance, it belongs to them by right as the sons of God, if children, says the Apostle, then heirs, heirs of God, and joint heirs with Christ. Now the Lord will see to it, that every one of his family shall come into possession of the inheritance, for the Lord will maintain the cause of the afflicted, and the right of the poor, Ps., cxl. 12. But how strange it seems when the promise and providence seem to clash. When God is pleased to speak a promise to the heart of a believer, it is that thereby he may be comforted concerning the trials and troubles which continually befall him on his onward journey through the dreary desert. If troubles without and within make his heart to ach, the word of promise coming direct from heaven into his soul makes it glad. Jeremiah found it so, "Thy words were found, and I did eat them; and Thy word was unto me the joy and rejoicing of my heart," xv. 16. On that word the soul builds up itself in sweet assurance that every part thereof will be accomplished. Thus David "I have hoped in thy word," a promise coming in like manner as Moses speaks of it "My doctrine shall drop as the rain, my speech shall distil as the dew ; as the small rain upon the tender herb, and as showers upon the grass, Deut. xxxii. 2.

It is God's testimony unto the soul, and such a soul has the threefold witness that John speaks of in him. For these are the three that bear record in heaven, the Father, the Word, and the Holy Ghost, and these three are one. This Word will be laid up in the understanding and affections as the jewel of divine mercy, more precious than life itself. The tongue will be loosed to speak of it with warmth of heart and affection. By that word the soul knows the Lord has thoughts of peace towards him. Thus the word to him is as sweet in the mouth of faith as honey afterwards bitter, Rev. x. 10. For death is sure to follow upon it. Clouds of adversity will eclipse the rays of light and peace that have so blessedly refreshed the heart, the darkness comes over the mind, and everything with which he is connected now appears working contrary to the word upon which he has built, in which he has rejoiced ; upon which he has hoped and has boasted therein ; what a

crook ? O, says the poor sinking mind, I have been deceived;
I have been trusting to a lie, God never spoke the word ; I
am now ashamed of my hope, what a fool I was to speak
of it, for the thing will never come to pass. But the Lord
goes on working seemingly contrary until all His former
peace and joy tumbles into ruins, then says the. Lord " I
will build up his ruins, and O, in what a wonderful manner
he performs his word in every step in providence and grace,
taking a backward direction, so it seems to our carnal reason
and yet in the end all comes right and straight according to our prayers, our wishes, His promise, His purpose, and
that to the joy of our heart and to the praise of the glory
of His grace.

FOURTHLY. Another crooked thing is the evil of the
heart, it is a loathsome, vile, detestable body of sin and death.
What different shapes and forms it assumes ! it entwines
itself in every thought, enters into every desire, creeps into
every prayer, is in every word. This leaven of wickedness
is in every corner, is with us in all hours asleep or awake,
actively insinuating itself, fettering every thought ; would
you be holy, then like the troubled sea it is casting up its
awful filth. Would you seek God by prayer ?   then, like a
flood, it will force its way in, sweeping every hallowed thought
from the mind. Would you listen to the word when in the
public means ? then like a thief it secretly enters, captivates
the mind, that you are so bewildered not to know anything
that has been said. Do what we will this evil principle will
work. This is indeed a crooked thing, and the thing itself
will never be made straight, it proceeds from the crooked
serpent, and will always remain crooked. Now God will
make the trial of this (crooked as it may be) straight.
There is in every Saint two distinct principles ; flesh and

spirit, life and death, enmity and love, the old man and the new, and these are continually at war. What changes we are the subject of in our spiritual warfare; now warm-hearted for a moment, cold the next, now for a time abasing ourselves in the dust, then exalting ourselves, fleeing from the world, now running after it. On our knees feeling shame and confused before God, then in a short space of time filled with pride and self-importance.

The spirit by these things leads us into the battle-field, that we might know the evil of sin and mourn on the account, and see the power of divine grace overcoming sin. The deeper we sink in self abasement, under the feeling of our vileness, the higher we rise in the sweet victory of grace. The blacker we look in our own eyes, the more precious will Jesus be to us. Thus the crook is made straight.

FIFTHLY. Another crook is the failure the believer often experiences, in not realizing in his attendance on the public means those precious things he promises himself, " How amiable are thy Tabernacles, O Lord of Host," is the language of the heart, when going to meet with the Lord's people, and that which is far more blessed, the Lord himself. The very sight of the people wending their way to the house of prayer seems to soften his heart, and for a moment the tear of gratitude to drop from his eye.

> How did my heart rejoice to hear
> My friends devoutly say,
> In Zion let us all appear
> And keep the solemn day.

With this feeling he enters the place which, by the presence of God, has been at times a Bethel to his soul; the house of God. But instead of his heart growing warmer, a strange feeling of dulness creeps over him; his mind is inactive, thus gradually he sinks out of all the pleasing sensations he felt on the road, into a carnal, dead, miserable state. Nor can he with all the effort he is master of prevent his thoughts roving first to one thing, then to another, until he is full of confusion, ashamed of himself. The service is lost to him not receiving any benefit, neither the hymns nor chapter read, prayer or sermon having made any impression. How confounding this is to him, and more so, if after the service, in converse with others he perceives their countenances shine, and he hears them tell how the service has been blessed to them, whilst he has been in a stupid, unfeeling, and miserable state.

The ordinance is of God, it is that which he has appointed and honoured many times with His spiritual gracious presence. Have I worshipped, says the soul, after due order ? it may be in something I have been walking contrary to God, and He has walked contrary to me. Sincerity springs up, and begins to make diligent search for the cause of such deplorable disappointment, and at the same time breathes out the fervent wish " Search me O God and know my heart, try me, and know my thoughts." And upon trial there appears many things, though hid in some secret corner, yet had an influence upon the soul, blunting the desire thereof, and causing such death in hearing. The idols of gold and silver and other things hidden in the chamber of imagery which are now brought to light, by the Lord, thus for a time stopping the sweet stream of his soul-reviving mercy. Thus so soon as discovered they are crucified.

Now the crook is made straight by the Lord shewing the soul that He is holy, and that nothing but holy men can appear before him with acceptance.

Fain would the heart unite
  A Christ with idols base ;
And link mid-day with night,
  Or Mammon foul with grace.
And in one bosom, false as hell ;
  Would have the Ark and Dagon dwell.

The last thing to notice, " I will break in pieces the gates of brass, and cut in sunder the bars of iron." We may be sure of this, that so far as the words relate to the victories of Cyrus they have long since been fulfilled. There is a spiritual meaning in them. A gate, in the strict sense of the word is that by which we are admitted into any place. We read of the gates of hell, " Upon this rock will I build my church ; and the gates of hell shall not prevail against it, Matt. xvi, 18.

The conclusion I come to is, that the power, craft, and policy of Satan will again and again attack the Church of Christ, and in assulting her will take many of her citizens prisoners, being taken captive by him, they are shut up within the strong gates of fear, guilt, and despair. Having no power to liberate themselves, neither can any friend gain access to them, to relieve them, the gates that shut them in that horrible darkness of mind shuts out every friend, every comfort, every promise, every ray of light, or if any light is admitted only sufficient to manifest the narrow limits of his cell. However, our precious Lord Jesus "Has the keys of of hell and death," Rev. i. 18., and when He opens, none can shut, He has the key of Redemption ; and the key of love. The Lord will break in pieces the strongest gates and bars, when the time comes to set his prisoners free. And spiritually, the Lord Jesus has broken the most powerful of spiritual bonds, and made us free indeed. Brass and iron are as straw before the flame of Jesus' love. Such of you as